Foreword

Some of these short stories were written over fifteen years ago. My passion for short story writing grew stronger when my English teacher, Mr. Leroy Pemberton, encouraged me to save one of my short stories because he felt that one day the short story would provide an income for me. I took my teacher's advice, and just as I completed college, I began writing short stories again with the intention to help young people who are facing adversities in life. I wanted them to know that I encountered my own challenges, but I never gave up, because God is at the center of my life, and whatever He can do for me, the Lord can do for them as well.

The story in the book entitled; "A Dream Come Through" is my own life experience, and I hope that many youths will be inspired by that story to do their best in school, no matter what the challenges are.

To the other readers, I hope that you also would be inspired by these short stories.

Remember this passage of scripture: **"I can do all things through Christ who strengthens me." (Philippians 4:13)**

"**Always humble yourselves before the Lord, and he will lift you up.**"

Contents

What Went Wrong………………………………………………….....5

Faith Unleashed……………………………………………………...10

A Dream Come Through……………………………………….14

A Cry For Help …...…………………………………………………18

An Answered Prayer……………………………………………...21

Can He Read The Sign…………………………………………….25

Forgiveness………………………………………………………….30

Out Of Desperation…..…………………………………………....37

Learning The Hard Way……..…………………………………….41

Out Of The Blue…………………………………………………….44

Pay Now Or Later…………………………………………………..47

Picking Up The Pieces………………………...……………………54

The Compassionate Grandmother………………………………..57

Hope On The Other Side………………………………………….60

The Coincidence…………………………………………………….63

Easy Come, Easy Go……………………………...……………….68

The Last Dollar……………………………………………………....72

The Bullies ………………………………………………………….79

Short Cut Home…………………………………………………….84

Gone So Long……………………………………………………….89

Gone, But Not Forgotten…………………………………………94

The Trainee Pilot…………………………………………………..98

What Went Wrong

The silence of dawn had broken into light. Samuel could not sleep.

All night he was trying to figure out why over the last few weeks, the gap of communication widened between his father and him.

Samuel sauntered around the block, away from his home, to ease his mind. For him, the buildings seemed endless and the streets were getting longer and longer. Yet the streets had not changed. They were wide and still shaded by rows of shrubs. The houses were still white with pillar fronts, and lustrous green lawns could still be seen.

"Perhaps it was my mind slipping away from reality," Samuel said.

Within a few minutes, a truck rushed past him, with a sudden roaring sound that made him leap out the street. The sound hit him Then he said, "My father's voice is like a tape recorder in my head. I could still hear my father's voice bombarding the small room in which I slept."

"You dumb mule-head you! You will never turn out to be nothing! You do not have what it takes to be somebody of good character. I do not know why I ever invested money in you!" His father had hardly taken a breath in all that time. Samuel remembered listening to the valleys of his fathers' abusive voice.

Then he bellowed, "What have I done to you, dad, to deserve this treatment?" His father had given him a penetrating look, and he wistfully walked out the room.

Samuel was shambling along the street with his hands in his trousers back-pockets, forcing his mind away from his present thoughts. He was focusing on going back home now.

When Samuel returned home from his walk, his father shouted, "Samuel, find somewhere to live!"

"Why dad?" Samuel asked in astonishment.

"I do not owe you an explanation, boy!" his father responded.

Samuel's anger mounted, and he turned away from his father. He walked a few frustrated steps and then turned back to face his father. "It was hard enough for you to treat me as if I am nobody, but now you want to throw me out the house?"

Eventually, his father put down his glass. He spoke to Samuel hastily and sarcastically. "What am I supposed to do? Say I changed my mind, boy?" The sarcasm in his father's voice was heavy. The word 'boy' came spitting out like the insult was intended to be. Then his father said, "I am surprised that your smoking pals cannot give you a bed to sleep on."

"I do not know what you are talking about, dad. Furthermore, my friends and I do not smoke."

"You do not what?"

"Yes, I do not smoke, dad," Samuel said with determination.

"Who do you think you fooling, boy?

Samuel was overcome by confusion. "But I swear that I am telling the truth, dad." He tried desperately to convince his father that he did not smoke. Samuel said, "Dad, if I used to smoke, you would have seen my eyes red, my white teeth turned brown, and nicotine on my fingers." The more Samuel talked, the dumber his father began to play and the more he did not believe him.

"But no so school children say." His father said sarcastically. Samuel's father was unmoved by Samuel's plaintiveness. Then his father took a cigar form his pocket and began to question him. "Why this cigar was in your school bag?" his father asked.

"I do not know, dad." Samuel's bewilderment was patent.

"Why is this cigar in your school bag?" his father repeated, the question more slowly, with exaggerated insulting patience.

"I do not know, dad."

His father was rapidly reaching a point of exasperation.

Suddenly, the doorbell rang. It was Samuel's school Principal, Mrs. John.

"I hope I have not come at a bad time, Mr. Jones."

"No, Mrs. John your timing is perfect." After another long pause, Samuel's father beckoned Mrs. John to come inside. The door remained half-closed. Samuel's heart was now pumping.

"I wonder why Mrs. John is here?" Carlos asked himself.

Then his father called him.

Samuel went speechless, before he could say a word. "I am coming, dad."

Now the time had come for Samuel to know why Mrs. John visited them. "Here I am, dad."

Then Mrs. John greeted Samuel with a smile, before she uttered a word.

"Samuel, as I was just telling your father," Mrs. John took a long pause before continuing. "It was brought to my attention that some students had placed some cigars in your school bag."

In the meantime, Samuel stared his father, straight in his eyes, as if he was trying to draw attention to his own veracity, which his father failed to acknowledge.

But his father tried to avoid Samuel's eyes, staring right at him.

"Samuel, I am deeply sorry for what had happened, and I can assure you and Mr. Jones that the matter will be dealt with promptly."

"So do you know the persons who are responsible for committing this offence, Mrs. John?" Samuel asked politely.

"Yes, Samuel. They are Joseph and Raul. I am not surprised about these boys' behaviour. They made sure that their message appeared to be right by twisting the facts and speaking lies and half-truths."

Samuel's father hesitated before he said, "Mrs. John, I am glad that this matter was brought to my attention. The way those boys did it, I was so convinced that my son was smoking. For the last few times, I acted on what I heard instead of finding out the facts."

Then Samuel's father nodded in a gesture of approval as Mrs. John said, "Your son is a boy with integrity, Mr. Jones."

Mr. Jones, in turn, said, "Yes, Samuel is a boy with integrity."

Then Mrs. John told them it was nice speaking to them, as she extended her hand to shake Mr. Jones' and his son's hands. After that, Mr. Jones escorted Mrs. John to the door and thanked her for coming by again.

The moral of the story: Find out the facts before you act.

Faith Unleashed

As Andy peeped out of his window, he saw the sun shining brilliantly over the meadow. Streaks of sunlight darted between the branches, and birds on the tree tops whistled melodiously.

After he had prayed to the Lord, the doorbell rang. As he opened the door, Andy was alarmed. His brother had a cigar in his mouth. The whitish-greyish thick puff of smoke smudged his brother's face. Andy was speechless. His face was as hard as steel. He took a few frustrated steps out the doorway. For a long time, he remained silent. Then he sighed. Tears began to leak down his cheeks.

"You look worried," his brother said.

"On second thought, I am glad that you came to my home," Andy said, half-sobbing, "It is not a question of being worried, it is a question of being concerned. It is not only the bad ones but the dumb ones that get sucked under." Andy hated staring at his brother. "As a youth, I was full of rage and resentment. My quick temper led to stormy outbursts of anger. I drank, smoked and led an immoral life."

"What does this have to do with me?" his brother questioned." I do not need you to tell me all this rubbish."

"I care for you my little brother. Nigel, I have been down that road you are heading." replied Andy. He smiled in a way that made Nigel feel he was in pain. "You never knew that, did you?"

"No," answered Nigel. "I truly did not know," he said, as he watched his brother with his eyes open wide.

"Oh, yes," Andy said as he nodded his head. "I used to hang out with other rebellious youths, and we drank and took drugs. At times, when I wanted to feel higher, I injected myself with heroin and anything else I could have gotten my hands on.

When I could not get the drugs, I used to break into people's house and I stole their things and sold them to get money to buy drugs."

Nigel was quiet and digesting what his brother was saying.

"Gradually, I realized that my so-called friends were associating with me only for what they could receive. After a while, I was feeling empty and frustrated, then I left my associates."

"So was there anything else that caused you to quit your life-style?" Nigel asked.

"Yes," replied Andy." I found a Bible on the street, and the very first scripture, when I opened the bible, was James (4:8). It says, ***"Draw close to God, and he will draw close to you."*** From that moment, I knew that the Lord wanted me to change to a personality that would be pleasing to him."

Nigel was now filled with his brother's life testimony.

"A growing knowledge of the Bible had redirected my course in life," Andy said in a soft voice.

Both of them walked away from the doorway and sat outside on the bench in the breezy yard. Nigel smiled. The cigar was now out of his hand. He was playing with his mouth and not looking at his brother. "I have been someone I did not recognize, I did not know that I could have been so misguided." Nigel paused looking inward. "I am not talking about it now because I feel guilty or anything of that nature. Maybe it would be better if I did. I really do not know." He held the cigar that was not burning now and rolled it between his palms. "Well, Andy, I needed to find a friend to lean on. I needed a quiet place and I could not find anything."

"Well, my brother, you came to the right person and the right place at the right time," answered Andy.

"I knew that everything I was doing was just locking me into it." Nigel abruptly dropped the cigar, looking at his brother with a small, still smile, then he hugged his brother with tightened arms.

"I could not tell you why I left home, in the first place," Nigel told his brother as he stood up and faced the window. "The reason why I left .... I was smoking very badly so I felt, if I left Dorset village, I would have a chance to pick up my life. But nothing changed except the fact that I was just older. I am really glad that I came to visit you. You made me realize that I have not gone too far to turn back."

"You are my brother," Andy said, staring directly at his brother and not smiling at all.

"Thanks brother, your testimony about your life shed light on mine," Nigel said with a smile as both of them gestured goodbye.

The moral of the story: Sharing your failures with others can inspire others to go on in life.

A Dream Come Through

As Sophia stood gazing at a few pin-top stars at almost vanishing point in the changing spirit of the sky, she wept hysterically. Then she threw her puny hands in the air. "Lord, my hope was to go to college (sixth form)," she cried as she said these words.

Immediately, she tossed herself on the thirsty earth. Then, with her clenched fist, she pounded and pounded the dusty earth. "Lord, why me! Lord why me! I tried, and still failed the matriculation standard for sixth form."

At once, Sophia scrambled to her feet. She hustled back into her bedroom. Her mouth was in a terrible grimace and tears were streaming down her cheeks. She gave no immediate reason for her tears. Her brother hoped that, as was the custom, she would favour him with an explanation.

Sophia cried herself to sleep. In between, when she woke up from her sleep, the examination results flooded her mind. Then she took some soursop-bush tea to help her back to sleep.

The next morning, Sophia told her brother the story. "Jamie, you know that going to sixth form was always my childhood dream."

"Yes," her brother answered with an open mind.

"Well, I passed six subjects in all, but not English. English is compulsory to attend Sixth Form College. Jamie, you know what even pained me until my bones ached? Many people said I will never make it any further than high school. I do not believe that."

"Sophia, whatever you put your mind to you can do it," Jamie said with confidence in his voice. For the next few days, Sophia was determined to pass her next English examination. She read more to improve her grammar and vocabulary. Then she tried desperately to find an English teacher.

Three months later, her search came to a halt. She found an enthusiastic teacher, Mr. Pemberton. Sophia was now attending his evening English class twice a week. The first lesson was on short story writing. Sophia hated to write short stories. However, she was willing to make a fresh start with writing short stories.

Sophia tried to follow her teachers approach. "Keep a note pad" was Mr. Pemberton's motto when it came to writing good short stories. She even copied his patient manner, and unconsciously she impersonated his voice. "You have to write down ideas from dreams, reminiscences and meditation. Read short stories, novels and extracts or excerpts."

Sophia encountered many challenges. But she was not put off. Six months afterwards, Sophia began improving in her English. She became quite skilled at writing short stories. The first story that she wrote in class, the tutor marked it and wrote "Excellent" at the bottom of the paper. From since that day, whenever Sophia sat down to practise her short stories, her face became almost angelic. It lit up with a kind of softness, concentration and pride. After a while, practising to write short stories became an obsession.

In June of the same year, Sophia sat the G.C.E 'O' level English Examination. She was confident that she would pass the examination. For the remaining months after Sophia wrote the English examination, she waited anxiously for her results.

Finally, in August, the results came back. Occasionally, a picture of not passing the English flashed across her mind, but she pushed it back into the subconscious. "I will pass my English and go to college." she said. The confidence she tried to put in her voice failed; it quaked a little. She eventually managed to convince herself that she would pass the English and go to college.

Then it happened!!! Sophia passed the 'O' level English. She was overwhelmed with joy. "I am going to sixth form! I am going to sixth form!" she said to herself as she screamed to the top of her voice.

In September, Sophia went for her college interview. She was accepted. Sophia's dream was alive. A smile appeared on her lips. Sophia was thrilled that the Lord and well-wishers helped her to fulfill her dream.

To this day, Sophia still keeps the short story at the bottom of which her tutor wrote "Excellent," even though she was finished with college.

The moral of the story: Never give up; fight to the very end.

A Cry for Help

Marylin squinted out the window as if to collect her last breath.

Her heart was beating out a heavy rhythm as her perspiration beaded her forehead. Just as she stepped into the living room, her father's eyes closed, and it appeared as though he was in a world all by himself. Marylin took a deep breath, then she said, "Dad, I failed."

For a moment, it was as though Mr. Clarke was just waking up from his world. "Marylin, what did you say?"

"Dad, I failed."

"You what! All that sacrifice I made, and you telling me you failed. No, Marylin, you just teasing me, because you want to upset me."

"No, dad, I failed."

"You know what? I should have followed my mind. All along I was saying that no matter what schooling you got, it still would not mean anything. And somehow you managed to convince me that I was right."

Marylin could not stand to see the pain in her father's face. She bowed her head as she bit her fingernails. "I am sorry, daddy," she said in a low tone of voice. Tears sprang from her eyes.

Her father's mouth twisted into a grimace.

"Marylin, I do not want to see you anywhere in my sight!"

She raced out the house until she reached Pinney's, beach which was a short distance from her home. She sat down on the sand under a coconut tree. She stared at the waves from far away, until they crashed upon the rocks. At times, the waves encroached upon the shore. Then she said to herself, "Well, my dad will get at least one of his wishes. He does not want to see me in his eyesight and I am going to make sure of that."

Marylin stood up and walked towards the sea as if there were no tomorrow. She continued to walk until the water reached under her neck. Then she swam out as far as she could. Then she said, "Doing something stupid, right now, is a permanent solution to a temporary problem." As she turned to make her way back to the shore, suddenly, she was afraid. She shivered, although she was not conscious of feeling cold. Then she saw beneath the surface of the water, the high dorsal fin of a shark, knifing through the water. Her teeth clenched and her eyes were wide with terror. She swam as fast as she could. Marylin was less than a quarter mile from the shore. The shark was cutting through the water, without wavering.

When Marylin reached the shallow water, she was thinking more clearly. She was full of resolution, but she had little faith. A swift current had set in around her. Despite all of the techniques Marylin used, the crest of the churning tide was against her. She cried out in despair, "Lord save me, I do not want to die now." Occasionally, the waves lifted and struck at one another, their crests hissed with spray. Marylin was surprised that the current caused the shark to drift away from her.

Within fifteen minutes, the shark circled back. Marylin was filled with terror. She fought on, anyway. At last Marylin crawled ashore. She was terrified and exhausted. She knelt down on the sand and prayed to the Lord for saving her life. Then she fell prostrate on the sand. There she lay as if she were dead.

The moral of the story: Kind or harsh words can determine someone's destiny.

An Answered Prayer

It was dull season, the time of the year when all the sugarcanes would have been harvested. At times, a mellow softness appeared to form an umbrella over the entire earth.

As Miss James spread the trash between her humming, she said, "Lord, have mercy upon me." In distress, she sobbed. Then she said, "In all my years, nothing upset me more than the fact that I could not finish school. At the age of fourteen, my mother died. I had to work to support my little brother and sisters. Lord, I do not want Sindy to sweat like me to put food on the table."

It was now midday. Miss James threw her hoe over her shoulder and held her lunch kit in the other hand. As she dragged her weary feet in the scorching sun, the narrow, pitched road glimmered with sunlight. Her only wish at that moment was a lift home. Gradually, her pace slackened, but she was determined to make it home.

Within a quarter of an hour, the rattling and groaning of a vehicle reached her ears. Minutes later, she spotted the vehicle in the distance. As the vehicle got closer, she realized it was Mr. Bagnal, the estate manager, who was also her neighbour.

He halted. "Miss James, do you want a lift?"

"Yes, bossy," she said, half-smiling. She then heaved her hoe and kit to the back of the jeep, and got in the front seat.

"So you going home?" he inquired.

"Yes, bossy," she said wearily. There was a good mile in front of them and it would be uncomfortable if the conversation ended there.

"So you going to take a long rest until tomorrow?" Mr. Bagnal asked.

"First thing I am going to do is cook," Miss James responded.

"My wife cooked plenty of food, so I do not know if you would like to stop by and have a meal with us."

"All right, bossy," Miss James said after making up her mind.

They were a few blocks away from his home now.

Mrs. Bagnal was just about finishing, arranging the table when she heard the jeep rumbling to a stop. She opened the door and greet them both.

Then Mr. Bagnal said, "Lou, I brought a guest for dinner."

"Come on, in I have plenty for all of us to eat," Mrs Bagnal said, smiling.

By now, Sindy was on her way from school. Every afternoon, after school, Sindy would head straight to Mrs. Bagnal's house for cookies. She would dash around the side of the house and then climb over the railings of the verandah.

As she stepped into the dining room, she saw her mom, and Mr. Bagnal and Mrs. Bagnal seated at the dinner table. Sindy pretended she was looking at the pictures on the wall, but she stole glances at her mom from the corner of her eyes. She knew her mother was talking about her. "Good-afternoon, everyone," Sindy said.

"Sweetheart, how was school?"

"Mom, school was fine."

Then Mrs. Bagnal pulled out a chair next to her, and indicate to Sindy and smiled. "Sindy, your mom was just telling us that you got all A's on your last report card."

"Yes," Sindy said, smiling happily.

There was an envelope on the dining table. Sindy knew something was on.

"Well Sindy," Mrs. Bagnal said, "I would like to give you this envelope." As Mrs. Bagnal extended her hands out to Sindy, she said, "Sindy I know that this will mean a lot to you."

As Sindy took the envelope, she smiled and said, "Thanks, Mrs. Bagnal."

Then she put it away.

But Mrs. Bagnal insisted that she opened it.

"I wonder what this paper is all about," Sindy asked herself. As she read it, her eyes lit up. It was a scholarship for her entire college tuition. Sindy hugged Mrs. Bagnal and thanked her and her husband for the scholarship.

Sindy's mother wept, and also thanked Mr. Bagnal and Mrs. Bagnal. Then she shouted praises to the Lord. "I was trying desperately to save some more money for Sindy's college education, but now both of you have blessed Sindy and me with this scholarship.I feel like an elephant just took its foot off my chest." Miss James was so overwhelmed, she just kept on saying, "Thank you, Thank you."

Then Mrs. and Mr. Bagnal said they were equally happy to give to someone they knew would appreciate such a generous offering.

When they arrived home, tears sprang to Miss. James's eyes. Then she knelt down and said, "Lord I knew you would answer my prayer, in due time. Thank you, Thank you, Lord."

The moral of the Story: When you least expect it, the Lord would use someone to help you with your burdens.

Can He Read The Sign?

It had been raining for well over an hour. Jason was walking through the driving sheets of rain. His wet blue jeans were rubbing him on the inside of his tights, while his wet shirt clung to him under the heavy, sodden of his blue jacket like a tight skin.

Jason was longing for shelter and something to eat. As he turned the corner, his eyes lit up and his mouth began to run water. He saw a sign board with a juicy hamburger on it. Jason burst into the place.

The bartender turned slowly, smiling. His teeth were very white. "My! My! My! What can I do for you, sonny boy?" The bartender asked.

"I need a soda and one of those juicy hamburgers," Jason said, smiling.

"That will be seven dollars and fifty cents," the bartender said.

Jason knew that the blue dollar bill he had was ten dollars. He took it out and paid the bar tender.

As he strolled away with the soda and the hamburger, the bartender called him back for his change.

Meanwhile, a stockily-built cowboy was watching Jason steadily. Jason just shifted under his stare. The cowboy stood up and walked a few steps towards Jason. The sound of his steel-tipped boots echoed in the high-roofed room. As he edged nearer to Jason, he said, "Don't you know that this place is just for cowboys?" He spoke deliberately in a high pitch manner.

Jason did not answer. He continued to eat his hamburger and drink his soda. Then the cowboy walked slowly around the table. The place was silent now. The barman knew that trouble was around the corner. In a mocking tone of voice, the barman heard the cowboy bellow to him, "What is this false cowboy doing in here?"

"I do not know, comrade," the barman replied quickly.

"Barman, what is this false cowboy doing in here?" The cowboy repeated the question with exaggerated, insulting impatience.

"I do not know, comrade," the barman again responded, looking steadily at the cowboy with his hand on his gun.

Suddenly, the cowboy burst out with laughter.

Jason rose suddenly, unsteadily, with his eyes on the cowboy.

Another cowboy in the extreme corner of the bar for a moment seemed moved by the strength of the argument. His expression registered a concession that the other cowboy might, after all, have a point. But he wished the cowboy would solve the problem differently.

Then the first cowboy started laughing again. "Boy, some boy, whom you left crying somewhere, must be crying for his jacket." The cowboy taunted Jason.

Jason watched him, with his face and eyes sharp with defiance, his body taut with deep hate.

"You cannot just barge in here and expect to get out of here, whole," the cowboy said with sarcasm in his voice.

Jason turned and looked towards the window. The rain had slacked to a drizzle. He was wishing that if he could have read, he would not have been in that place. Eventually, he said to himself, "Well, I will have to fight my way out."

Immediately, the boy sprang forward. He locked his right arm around the cowboy's neck, and seized his gun.

Within a few minutes, the cowboy muttered, "In here is hot like a furnace." He pulled his handkerchief from his shirt pocket.

To Jason's surprise, the cowboy pulled out a gun. Then he said, "False cowboy, I will give you a chance to shoot me. On the count of three, "the faster man wins."

Instantly, Jason surrendered. He knew that there was no way he could outdraw the cowboy. Jason dropped the gun. The cowboy advanced.

"You jerk!" he said in a high pitch voice.

The barman shouted to the cowboy. He was rapidly reaching a point of exasperation. He racked his brain for the best arrangement of words to meet the situation.

"Put the gun down, please. Someone could get hurt. You can solve this problem differently. Put the gun down, please." "A wave of sadness came over the barman. He could not get to the cowboy. The cowboy was now breathing heavily. In the blink of an eye, the cowboy rammed Jason's head against the wall. Jason's body shook. His hands trembled. He choked a little.

Then, a lanky cowboy stood behind the stocky one, imploring, whispering: "Please, give the boy a chance." Instead, the cowboy put the gun to Jason's head.

Jason sobbed hysterically. In between his tears, he said, "Please give me a chance. I cannot read. I only saw the hamburger sign on the board. I was really hungry and cold."

Before Jason could utter another word, the cowboy pulled hard on the trigger. The hammer hit the barrel with a loud click. Jason jerked. The cowboy pulled again on the useless trigger. The cowboy's eyes were wild, wide and terrified now.

As the cowboy pulled the trigger fiercely, it clicked and clicked. He was furious now. The gun was not doing what he wanted. Suddenly, the cowboy felt a great burning pain in his chest. He screamed and whimpered and screamed again. With his final despairing shout, he flung the gun away.

With his fingers and arms spread out, mouth in a terrible grimace, eyes light up and burning, he tried to leap on Jason.

Jason shifted his body and ducked his head.

The cowboy slammed straight on the wall and fell backwards. His forehead, lips and nostrils were slowly dripping blood. He was unconscious.

While the people were worrying about the cowboy, Jason slipped through the door.

From that day, Jason vowed to go to evening literacy class, not only to be able to read signs, but also to fulfill his dream as a mechanic.

The moral of the story: Education can empower an individual to make wise decisions in life.

Forgiveness

The awakening of dawn sprawled over the land, painting a screen on the trees. Toya was tossing and murmuring in her bed. She was still furious with her mother. "How mama could forgive that so-called man, called my father? Every day he battered mama. Every year mama was hospitalized, and most of the time she had to undergo surgery. Mama's abdomen alone looked like a railway line. You know the thing that made me angry most of the time? No matter how many times he blacked up mama's eyes, she always found some lame excuse why he did it to her. I wondered whom she thought she was fooling?"

The deeper Toya's annoyance mounted, the louder she got, when recalling some of mama's lame excuses. "Mama, why he beat you?" she asked.

"I forgot to iron your father's shirt, I forgot to sew his pants, I forgot his food on the stove, and it dried out a little; Oh and I forgot to give him half my salary," her mother said.

"Nonsense! That doesn't give him the right to beat you, mama, as if you are a punching bag. Come on, mama. You really want me to forgive that abuser?"

Toya soon heard her mother's voice bombarding the small room in which she slept. "Get up! Get up! Get up! You think the morning is waiting on you?"

Then her father intervened and said, "Girl, you come here. You too lazy. I do not expect nothing good from that girl." Toya's father had hardly taken a breath in all that time.

She listened to the valleys of her father's surging voice. Then Toya chuckled before she grumbled, "I had been awake for about four hours now, even before they were up and about. He is always controlling instead of being loving."

Toya then gave a final heave out of her bed. She knew her father had left for work. Toya strolled downstairs. As she was a yard away from the dining room, she let her shoes clatter on the tiles to announce her approach. As she entered the room, her pace slackened. With just a few more steps, Toya pulled the wooden chair from under the matching table, hastily. Then she took a piece of ham and chewed it for two minutes. Seconds later, Toya squashed the food together, making roads and patterns. When she was bored of doing that, she drew pictures in the food. Secretly, Toya passed chunks of food to the cat.

Just then, Toya's mother, Tina Adams, turned around. She complained, "Toya, you know how much time I spent preparing breakfast!"

Toya snarled, "You worry about the time you spent preparing food, but you allow yourself to be my so-called loser father's punching bag."

Then her mother replied, with her eyes looking wild like a lion, "Never disrespect your father like that!" Her mother shouted as she gave Toya a back-hand slap.

Toya fixed her mouth in a terrible grimace. Instantly, she tossed the poached egg across the room. It landed on her mother's face. Then Toya said, "That serves you right."

As her mother tried desperately to clear her face, she sprung forward, locked her right arm around Toya's neck. The chair clattered to the floor and the table was overturned as they wrestled on the floor.

Toya was breathing heavily. Her mother had the upper hand. Mrs. Adams turned to the stool and pressed her hand against the edge with her body. Suddenly, her mother's hand trembled. She did not want to physically hurt her daughter. Then she said, "Toya, I do not like how you are handling your anger. We can work it out in a civilized manner." Then she eased Toya away from her.

Soon after, the doorbell rang. Her mother picked her way gingerly to the door. Then she peeped through a little glass window. The person was her pastor; Pastor John. Mrs. Adams rushed to the nearest mirror. She tried to fix her hair, and make it appear as if she was not just in a fight with her daughter. Within seconds, she rushed back to the door. Mrs. Adams opened the door with a smile all over her face.

The pastor took off his hat. Then he greeted Mrs. Adams. Within seconds, the pastor said in a low tone of voice, "Mrs. Adams I do not mean to be rude. Your blouse is stained with something yellowish."

The pastor's words hit Mrs. Adams. Instantly, she remembered that some of the poached egg dripped down on her blouse during the altercation with her daughter.

As Mrs. Adams tried to think of some excuse, Toya just blurred out, "We had a fight."

Mrs. Adams bent her head.

Then the pastor said, "Well, we need to sit down and talk out this problem because it is no way to live." As the pastor sat down on the couch, he said, "Mrs. Adams, can you tell me what is the problem?"

"Well," Mrs. Adams said, and paused. Then she continued. "My-my-my-husband would beat me, and sometimes I have to end up in the hospital. Every time my husband did that to me, my daughter would get angry. Now it reached to the point that she is acting out her anger. She acted out worse when I told her that, as bad as the situation was, she has to forgive her father, and then move on with her life.''

"Okay, Mrs. Adams," Pastor John said. "Now Toya, what you have to say about this problem?"

"Pastor, I hate when my father abuses my mama emotionally and physically. All mama will say is that it is her fault why he beat her. On top of all that, she wants me to forgive him," Toya said, with a frustrated and disappointed look.

In a calm and reasonable way, the pastor said, "I understand what you are saying about your father's behaviour. However, what I do not agree with, is that you do not want to forgive him. As it is stated in the Bible, 'If you do not forgive one another, our Father in heaven will not forgive you.' Another reason you should forgive anyone who has done you wrong; you will not be bitter, thus you will not have actions that result in destructive behaviour. You understand what I am saying, Toya?"

"Yes, Pastor," Toya said.

"Now back to you Mrs. Adams. There are four basic needs in a relationship: Acceptance, Identity, security and purpose. To start with, Toya needs to know that she is accepted and appreciated in your family."

"So pastor, how can I give that to her?" Mrs. Adams said.

"You can use words of affirmation such as, 'Toya I am glad to have you as part of my family', 'or you mean the world to me.' Make sure every word you say you mean it in order for your words to make a positive impact," the pastor said.

"Okay pastor, from now on I will start making Toya feel accepted in the family. I guess why I never made Toya feel accepted is that when I was growing up, my family never made me feel accepted. As a result, of that I have a hard time expressing myself in that way to my daughter," Mrs. Adams said.

"Well, to start, it will be a little difficult, but as time goes on, it will be easier for you to do," Said the pastor.

Meanwhile, the expression on Toya's face was as blissful as if she had already arrived in the happy family of her dreams.

As the pastor noticed that he was getting through to the mother and daughter, he said, "Secondly, Toya needs to know that she is accepted for who she is and not what other people want her to be, then you must help her to strive on her strengths and help her to build on her weak areas in life."

Mrs. Adams shook her head in agreement with the pastor.

"Thirdly, Toya needs to know that you and her father are looking out for her safety. She needs to feel that you are caring for her at all times, not because it is your duty to look out for her, but because you love her. Finally, Toya needs to know that she is created by God for a purpose," the pastor said.

"How do I know what is her purpose?" Mrs. Adams asked inquisitively.

"Well, Toya is always helping little children with their homework and reading them stories that she wrote herself. Right there, Toya could become a teacher or an author that doesn't mean she is limited to those two worthy professions," Pastor John said.

By now both mother and daughter were smiling sweetly as their eyes met with one another.

"Mrs. Adams," Pastor John said, as he was moved by the eye contact between Mrs. Adams and her daughter, "do you know that people communicate their love by using one of the five languages of love?"

"What are the five love languages, Pastor?" Mrs. Adams asked.

"The five languages of love are: words of affirmation, gifts, spending time, touching, and doing service for others. To start with, words of affirmation. This deals with expressing love using positive words such as 'you make my life happy or I love the way you care for your family.' For others buying them a gift to make them feel loved; it does not have to be something expensive," he said.

"On the other hand, sometimes you will hear someone say that he or she wants to go biking or to the beach. They are telling you that they want to spend quality time with you," the pastor said.

"Toya is that type of person. She is always telling me that she wants to go shopping for clothes with me," Mrs. Adams said.

"Well, no matter how busy you are, spend the quality time with her," the pastor said.

"Another language of love is touching. Some people like to be hugged, or be patted on the back," the pastor said.

"Oh, as you said that, pastor, I noticed that when I pat my husband on the back, he seemed to be more loving," Mrs. Adams said.

"Well, touching might be his primary love language. So give him more touching," the pastor added.

"Finally, doing services for others. This might be in the form of taking out the trash or cleaning up after each meal. Toya, help your mother do the chores around the house," he advised.

"I will, pastor," Toya said, smiling whilst she was speaking.

Then the pastor said, "I would like to say a prayer for your family, Mrs. Adams."

"Yes pastor go right ahead."

"Father God, I came to You in agreement with the Adams' family. Lord, bless them with joy and everlasting love. When there are problems, Lord, let them solve these problems peacefully. Touch their hearts with compassion when they are hurting. Let them know that by leaning on You, they can conquer all things, Amen."

"Thanks be to, God," Mrs. Adams and her daughter said together

Gradually, the pastor rose from the couch. Mrs. Adams then escorted him to the door and thanked him for helping her family.

Then Pastor John said, "See you and your family in church next Sunday," as he bade farewell.

The moral of the story: It is better to forgive than to hold on to hurt.

Out Of Desperation

The wind twisted as it encroached upon the land. Troy was enfolded in the cushion of mist.

That morning, Troy missed the school bus. He had to walk to school. He strolled down the dusty road, which was bordered with cane fields. He was grumbling and mumbling to himself. Then he said, "If only I had stretched out my feet a little longer, I would have been on that bus."

Eventually, Troy took out some cookies from his lunch pack and munched on them. Occasionally, he drifted from one side of the road to the other, forcing his mind from his present predicament. As he passed the junction in the road that led to the Anglican Church, he lingered a bit.

Within an hour, Troy spotted a vehicle coming in the distance. He stood in the middle of the road with his hands up in the air.

As the driver approached him, he swerved away from Troy, who had dropped his hands to his side. The car halted a yard in front of Troy. Then the driver, with gloves on his hand, beckoned him to the waiting car. The driver asked Troy, as he get to the car, "Where are you heading?"

"To school, sir," answered Troy.

"Hop in," the driver said.

Soon, the car sped along the main road. Troy was sitting in the back seat. All kinds of thoughts flashed across Troy's mind. He was now frozen with terror. "I wonder what he is thinking? Since I got in the car, there has not been a sound!"

Troy was now a few blocks away from the school. He was overjoyed. But the driver sped up instead of slowing down. Troy was breathing fast, as if he was on a race track. Then, in between the rhyming of his heart beats, he shouted, "Stop here, please!" Then he yelled a second time, "Stop here!", but the driver did not utter a word as he dashed past the school.

The driver drove the car for well over three miles before he pulled over on the other side of the winding dirt road. Then he said, in a gruff voice "I just want to get some music tapes from under the seat." Troy was very suspicious, as a lot of musical tape swum in a semi-circle in the roof of the car.

"So why he could not pick one from there?" Troy asked himself.

The driver took out, not tapes, but a gun. Then he said to Troy, "Showtime." With a blink of his eyes, the driver pointed a gun at Troy's chest. At that moment, all Troy could have thought about was that he was not ready to die. His pulse quickened.

At the last moment, the driver turned fully around to keep his eyes on the road. A big truck that was loaded with sand was directly in his lane.

Troy screamed and shouted, "Mommy! Mommy!"

The driver panicked. He applied the brakes, but it only made the matter worse. The car picked up a skid and ran off the road.

Troy was trapped in the back seat .The only way out was to smash the glass to get out. As he surveyed the car, he tried to look for an object that was within reach and heavy enough to smash the glass. There was nothing visible on the seat. So he stretched his hand under the seat and he felt something like a spanner. He pulled it from under the seat to smash the glass to free himself.

All this time, the driver was trying to free himself as well.

As Troy smashed the glass he hustled out of the car, then he ran as fast as he could. When he peeped back over his shoulder, he saw the driver chasing him. Troy ran in front of a coming car, forcing the driver to come to a standstill. It was his uncle, Joe, Troy jumped in and his uncle sped away.

It was days later, Troy's uncle told him that the man who was chasing him was an escaped prisoner.

The prisoner was soon recaptured, had a retrial, and he was sentenced to life imprisonment.

The moral of the story is: Do not be quick to trust strangers.

Learning The Hard Way

The memories of Tim Harvey's grade school were still clear in his mind, although it was forty-odd years ago. As Mr. Harvey was strolling down George Street, with his hands in his pockets, half-smiling to himself, he said, "Boy, mama gone, but she moulded me into the person I am today." Tears began to flow down his cheeks. At first he made no effort to stop the tears from his face. Within a few minutes, he took his handkerchief from his pocket and mopped up his tears. He nodded his head and said again, "Boy, mama gone, but she moulded me into the person I am today."

Mr. Harvey walked on, slowly, until he reached the remains of his now broken-down primary school. The remains of the school were covered with wild flowers. Some of the flowers withered, and others folded their pedals within themselves in the heat of the day.

For a moment, Mr. Harvey sat down on some dry mango leaves that formed a crisp carpet under his feet. As he examined the mango tree bark, he saw what read "*T.H. and C.B*", engraved in the tree.

He could hardly believe his eyes. The initials he had notched out as a child could still be seen. He began to wonder what C.B. stood for. In his mind, he saw a picture of him. Then he giggled to himself and shouted, "Charles Browne! Charles Browne!"

Slowly, his mind drifted away, "I wonder what part of the world Charles Browne is, if he is still alive?" Then he chuckled to himself for a while, "Boy, I remember when mama taught me a lesson. When I was in six grade, she usually gave me my lunch kit and my little spending money, to buy my tamarind balls and sugar cake at break time.

One day she packed my lunch, as usual, and she said, "Son, read James 3:5 at break time for me." I said, "Okay mama, I will." When break time came, I didn't see my pocket money in my bag. I stood under the same mango tree, very sad. Then I said, "Maybe mama forgot to put my money in my bag." That same day when I got home from school mama called me and asked, "Tim did you read the Bible at break time?"

"Yes, mama," I replied.

The next day mama did the same thing. I did not find any money. I was mad and I cried when I saw that all the other children were eating their sugar cake. As I got home I said, "Mama these days you have not been putting any money in my bag."

Mama turned to me and said, "Son, read Philippians 4:13." As usual, she packed my lunch in my bag, but I did not find my money.

I told my mama, "Everybody is eating their sugar cake and I have none."

Mama said, "Tim, read Romans 12:1."

I told her, "Okay," but I never read it. By the end of the week I was so angry. I went back to my mama and I said, "Mama for the whole week I did not get any sugar cake or jaw- bone breakers."

Mama listened keenly then she said, "Tim, did you read your Bible?"

"Yes, Mama," I replied.

Mama paused, then she said, "Tim if you were reading your Bible you would have been able to buy yourself all the sugar cake in the world."

I looked at my mama as if she was going out of her head. Then she said, "Each passage from the Bible I told you to read, would have had a note, telling you where to find your money in your bag." "Now you have lost every cent." she said. At first I thought my mama was treating me badly, but now I looked back I can say, "Thank you mama, for loving me."

The moral of the story is: The truth will set you on the right path.

Out of the Blue

The blazing sun was so hot, it turned white. For a moment, it was as though Daniel was cast in gold. His eyes dazzled in the light. He always wore a broad brim hat to shield his face, which was lean and burned from his forehead to his firm tapering chin.

It was customary for Daniel on Saturdays to do his weekly shopping at J and T's supermarket.

People were shuffling in and out the supermarket. As Daniel completed his shopping, he joined a long queue of people waiting at the cashier's desk to be served.

Daniel heard a car screech to a halt. A short silence followed. To his surprise, four black-masked men burst through the door. Daniel trembled. His teeth were knocking each other.

Then a muscular masked man, who was wearing trousers which was made from a serge material, tucked into tall boots with metal reinforcement tips, ordered, "Everyone, stay where you are and no one will be hurt!"

The muscular masked man was eyeing the manager in an unfriendly way. Then he said, "What you fool think you are doing?" As he shook his head, he burst out with laughter. "Fellow, what are you going to do with that toy in your hand?"

"Just what you would use it for," the manager answered.

The masked man brandished his gun, then said, "This baby in my hand is the real thing."

Within ten minutes, a police car siren was heard in the distance. In a matter of a short time, the police took up position around the entire building.

The masked man realized there was no way out for him. He took a female customer and held her hostage. His frightened eyes which appeared from under the hat brim, glanced across the room. The second masked man, who was above medium height, stood in the door way. Then a third masked man, who was lanky, demanded that the cashier hand over all the money in the cash register, while the fourth masked man, who was stocky, pointed the gun at the cashier, whose heart was pounding rapidly. The customers froze in their tracks. Then an eerie silence crept over the room for a few minutes.

Suddenly, three of the men rushed out of the door, with bags upon bags of dollar notes and coins. They jumped into a waiting car. The fourth masked man, who was carrying all coins, was ambushed by Daniel. Daniel pushed one of the shelf of goods down on the masked man. In a flash, one of the customers seized the gun that was flung out of the masked man's hand, as he fell to the floor. He was trapped under the shelf. He struggled and struggled until he managed to free himself from the self. In a split second, he took another gun from his waist as he made an attempt to exit the door. The police men from all angles of the building were pointing their guns directly at him.

The police could not shoot. The masked man held the hostage closer to him. One of the police officers got on the hallo phone and said, "Mister, please let the lady go and no one will be hurt."

The masked man warned, "If any one of you makes an attempt to shoot, this lady will be a dead lady." The poor lady's heart was beating as if any minute it would explode.

Occasionally, the masked man would point the gun at the lady's head and threatened her that if she only moved, she would be dead. The lady made an attempt to pray, but she could not concentrate. She kept thinking that any minute she would be dead. Her mind flashed to her three small children. Then she began to sob.

Hours passed by and nothing changed, then finally the masked man surrendered. He released the lady on the side walk and flung his gun in the air. The police closed in on him. He was shackled and then taken to a waiting police car.

The moral of the story is: Anything can happen at anytime.

Pay Now or Later

As the silence of dawn broke into light, Jasmine's heart was thumping with anxiety. She had a serious decision to make.

Dismay filled her. She groaned quietly to herself. "What am I going to do?" Then, pulling herself together, she began quarreling with herself. "Jasmine," she said, "stop trembling and being scared. You have been sneaking out the house, and sooner or later you would have to pay for your action. Do not panic. Do not panic! Just think." She got up and set about her evacuation plan. Jasmine then gathered all her belongings together.

As usual, Jasmine and her mother ate breakfast, and her mother went to work afterwards. After preparing herself for school, Jasmine wrote her mom a note.

Dear mom,

I am sorry that I have to leave like this. I have a decision to make and I need some time, alone. Please, mom, do not make any attempt to find me. When I am ready I will find some means to contact you.

Love,

Jas

Jasmine dropped the note in front of the door mat and locked the door. Then, with some level of sadness, Jasmine put the key under the flower pot. Although it was hard for her, Jasmine bade farewell to the only home she ever knew. Jasmine took three awkward steps from the house. Eventually, she muscled up the courage and she quickened her pace, until the house was but a speck in her eyes.

That morning, Jasmine reached school very early. She opened her locker and put all her belongings in it.

At lunchtime, Jasmine ate with her best friend, Gresha. When Gresha asked Jasmine if she was all right, rather than opening up to her friend, Jasmine just said she was fine.

But Gresha gave Jasmine an awkward moment when she said, "I saw you come school very early, and normally you are late. You were carrying a lot of luggage."

"Luggage, Gresha?"

Gresha grinned, "Yes, luggage, Jasmine,"

Jasmine thought fast, "Oh, that Gresha. That is some of my clothes, I am going to spend the weekend with my auntie."

As school finished at half past three, Jasmine left, laden with her luggage, for the bus stop. It was about six o'clock, but Jasmine did not catch a bus. She began clinching her fist and occasionally crossing from one end of the road to the next. When she got tired of doing that, she stood near her luggage shifting her weight from one foot to the other.

Eventually, she saw a vehicle coming in the distance. As it drew closer and closer, she realized it was a bus. The bus stopped. Jasmine sighed with a relief. Then she got on the bus.

While Jasmine was travelling on the bus, she knew that it was the most testing part of the day she had to face.

Within half an hour, Jasmine stopped the bus. She got off the bus with her luggage, then she crossed the road to her friend's house. Jasmine, opened the gate and left her belongings in the yard. She went around the back of the house and found her friend Janice scrubbing her pots.

Janice turned and saw Jasmine. She smiled and said, "Hi, Jas. I am finished with your dress, did you coming for it?"

"No, Janice," she responded in a low tone of voice.

"So what is going on?"

Jasmine hesitated for a moment and then she decided to pitch. "I got a bit of a problem, Janice."

"Would you like a glass of lemonade to cool you down?"

"No, thank you, Janice."

"So let me hear your problem. There must be some way or another I can help."

Jasmine hesitated again for a moment and then blurted out, "I need a place to stay for a while. I thought you might be able to help me."

Janice smiled and said, "I am your friend, and that is what friends are for. I am going to lend a helping hand under one condition, that you answer my question.

"What is that, Janice?"

"Why do you want to sleep here and you know your mom does not like you doing that?"

"No, my mom does not normally let me sleep at your house. It's just that........" Jasmine did not like telling a lie to Janice, but she did not want to tell Janice about her pregnancy, at least now. "Well, my mom said that it was okay to spend the weekend with you."

"It is alright with me, as long as it is okay with your mom."

Half-smiling and half thoughtful, Janice begged Jasmine to give her a straight answer to her question. "You want to give me a straight answer to a straight question, Jas?"

"Of course, Janice."

"Well, then Jas, please listen carefully. I am someone who likes to mind my own business. Yes, I do not always go by the book, but I made and still make mistakes in my life. Do you understand what I am talking about, Jas?"

"I understand, Janice."

"Well I am glad you understand, because I would not want to assist anyone who, had say, sneaked out the window late at night, or skipped classes. These are the types of people I have a difficult time helping. So can you give me a straight answer Jas? Have you ever done anything, like what I just spoke about?"

Jasmine hesitated. She liked Janice, who, at times, was like a mother to her. Jasmine did not want to lie to her.

Jasmine said, "I sneaked out of the house a few times. Also, I skipped a few classes when I did not do my homework, but I never did anything very bad."

Janice nodded. "Well, you can sleep in the spare room."

That night Jasmine was very restless. It was as if a cloud had fogged her thought for a moment. "I know I have to tell my mom, but I do not know how to break the news to her. Worse yet, if mom finds out about my pregnancy, I should be the one to tell her," Jasmine said in a stressful way.

The next day, early, Jasmine telephoned her mom to let her know that she was planning to come home.

"Hi, mom."

"Jas, is that you? I am worried sick about you. Are you all right?"

"I am fine, mom."

"Where are you, Jas?"

"Mom, I am at Janice's."

"Jas, when are you coming home?"

"Mom, do not worry, I am packing my stuff to come home today."

"Ok Jas. I hope to see you real soon."

"I love you, mom." "Bye, mom."

"I love you, Jas." "Bye."

That day, Jasmine thanked Janice for her generous assistance.

Janice drove Jasmine home to her mom.

At last, Jasmine's mom heard a car pull up in front of the house. Then she said, "Thank God." Normally Jasmine's mom would have persuaded her that she was very angry. Then she would have hurriedly got a stick, sat down on a chair within the door and waited for Jasmine. This time she had a change of heart. Instead, she dashed out to caress her daughter as she thanked Janice.

As Janice drove off, Jasmine sobbed, hiding her head in her mother's bosom.

Her mom squeezed her and told her that everything would be alright. Then her mother helped her daughter with her luggage inside. After her mother stooped down, to put down the luggage, she raised Jasmine up and began kissing her, crying at the same time with tears in her eyes. Then she said, "When I began reading, my heart leaped. As I continued to read the note I cheered up a bit until I eventually cooled down. Jasmine, you know the greatest comfort I had?"

"What is that, mom?"

"I knew no matter what the problem was, you will not do something that you would deeply regret."

"Thanks mom, for having so much confidence in me."

"Now Jas, let us get down to your problem. Jas, please tell me what your problem is."

Jasmine hesitated a bit before saying a word, then she admitted "Mom, I am pregnant." Then she began to cry profusely.

Her mother broke down in tears also, as she hugged her daughter. Then her mother said, "I am ashamed of myself. I should have been there for you, but instead I kept on insulting you."

Eventually, her mother calmed down and she burst out with laughter. "I guess that the lime has not dropped far from the tree. Jas, there is something I never told you. When I was about your age, sixteen, I got pregnant and ran away. I did not know what to do. I was very lucky that my aunt took me to live with her until I reached of age to look after myself. The same way I treated you it was the same way my mother used to treat me. Jas as bad as the situation might seem to be, it brought some good with it. It made me realize that I have to be more like a mother to you."

Then Jasmine said, "Mom, I am sorry I ran away, and I thank you for not coming down on me."

"Jas, you will feel terrible and guilty for now, but eventually you would be able to learn from your mistake and move on. Jas, I am sorry that I just started speaking to you like a mother should. I'd hope one day you will come to forgive me."

"Mom, I am partly to blame, so do not get down on yourself. "

Then both of them vowed to each other that they would support one another in good times and bad times.

The moral of the story is: Think of the consequence of your actions before you take a leap.

Picking Up The Pieces

Genette sat alone on the verandah, looking at the beaming sunlight streaming through the trees. The nearby birds concealed themselves behind the bushes with restrained sounds.

As Genette sipped her morning tea, she thought to herself, "How could I ever confide in my friend, Rena, again? I felt embarrassed and betrayed yesterday, when Rena divulged something that we discussed in private. I used to feel a sense of emotional support, especially when I felt her mutual care, trust and respect. Now I really do not know what to really think of her. I do not even know if at that moment, she thought for a second that her attitude would have been humiliating for me. I do not even know if I will ever speak to her again."

Suddenly, Genette felt a hand tap her on her shoulder. She turned around quickly. It was her friend, Rena. "I could not believe that you had the energy to show your face here!"

"But, Genette, we are friends."

"After what you did yesterday, you still consider yourself my friend? A friend is supposed to be somebody you can rely on and trust, no matter what."

Rena bowed her head and murmured, "Gene, I came to apologize to you."

"Well, save your breath, because I do not want to hear what you have to say." Genette slammed the door and went inside the house.

In the meantime, Genette was observing Rena through the window. She was very solemn, biting her fingernails. Then she said to herself, "If Rena did it intentionally, she would not have come all this distance and still be waiting outside. Furthermore, if I continue to react rashly, will the situation ever be resolved?"

After considering the situation, Genette opened the door, and there was Rena, still waiting. "Rena, I guess because I am the victim of what took place yesterday, I merely reacted on the spur of the moment. But, I really trusted you and you let me down."

"Gene, I am truly sorry, I pray that the storm will pass without destroying our friendship."

"Since you have been straight and honest with me, we could pick up the pieces. "Deal, Rena?"

"Deal we have, Gene."

Both of them were now beaming with laughter. They caressed each other and went into the house.

The moral of the story is: If someone tells you something in confidence, do not broadcast it to others.

The Compassionate Grandmother

The afternoon began to lose its last vivid colour. The splendid gold spun into silver, and the silver was stained by the haze of dusk.

Shana was strolling home, all unconcerned, from piano class. Suddenly, she heard the sound of a siren in the distance. "I wonder what is going on?" she asked herself. "I just don't know."

Within five minutes, the fire truck was in sight. It was a few yards from her now. As the fire truck dashed passed it, left a small tornado behind it. She was all covered in the dust. Then Shana started to walk briskly.

About five minutes later, Shana was approaching the junction in the road that led her directly to her home, with cane fields on both sides. When she looked directly ahead of her, she saw a black puff of smoke climbing into the air.

She was galloping like a horse now. "My grandmother was all alone." she said in a panicking voice. The black smudges of smoke and trash painted the air. As far as she could see, everything was black like charcoal.

As she turned the corner where her grandmother lived, she saw a crowd of people, like bees on a hive. "Lord, I pray that my grandmother is all right; she is the only one I have!" Shana cried. Venturing closer to the scene, she saw the firemen busy quenching the blazing house fire.

Her heart was racing through her nostrils. She bore through the crowd and tried to rush her way into the house.

But a lanky fireman grabbed her with a firm grip and said, "You can't go in there, the house is on fire."

"My grandmother is in there" she said as she sobbed hysterically.

The fireman said, "Calm down. Everything is all right. Your grandmother is safe."

"Where is she?" begged Shana. "I need to see her, I need to see her now!"

The fireman responded, "She is over by the neighbour."

Shana plunged through the crowd, and rushed over by her grandmother. She pulled the door knob with all her might, and went racing into the house. "Granny! Granny!" she cried. Then she heard her grandmother's soft voice, and ran straight at her and hugged her. She sobbed and said, "Granny, you are alive!" as though she thought that she was dead.

She knelt down and said, "Lord, thanks a million for sparing granny's life!"

The moral of the story is: Love and compassion help to create and keep a bond in the family.

Hope on the Other Side

It was a relief for me when the doctor finally hustled into the room, with his briefcase clutched to his body. I eyed him until he bolted his office door.

Within fifteen minutes, the doctor was back out of his office. He moved swiftly to the front desk and called the first patient's name on the list. My heart jerked. I knew that I was next.

Suddenly, the thought of being terminally ill flashed in my mind. I had been to other doctors, but still I did not know exactly what my problem was. Momentarily, I was stiffened with nerve. Then I said, "You will be all right. Whatever is your problem, the doctor might not be able to fix it, but the Lord will." Gradually, my fear was conquered.

As I surveyed the waiting room, some of the patients were reading books or newspapers from the small center table. Others were seated as if the immediate thing on their mind was to see the doctor. There was a puny boy, who was sitting next to a man about in his mid-fifty's, whom I assumed was his father. Every minute, the boy would either climb onto the soft back long chair or cling to the man. Occasionally, the man would set his paper work aside and caress and stroke the little boy, the way a caring father would do. Then the man whispered something to the little boy and he giggled. Afterwards, the man went back to his activity.

The doctor was out of his office again. I knew that it was my turn now. My pulse quickened. I managed to stifle my emotions. Then the doctor called my name. I picked my way towards the office door, a bit nervous. As I closed the door behind me, I tried not to get ahead of myself. Then the doctor indicated to me to take a seat.

"How may I help you?" he said in a professional tone of voice.

Immediately, I began outlining my problem, along with the symptoms. After listening to me attentively, he rose from his seat to examine me. He paused. Panic engulfed me. Then he told me that it was acid reflux. I sighed. It was not the best news, but part of me was still happy that it was not life threatening. "Thank God," I said to myself.

As the doctor wrote the prescription, he related to me in a therapeutic way, which even reassured me that I would be alright. By the time he escorted me to the door, my mind was at ease. Then I paid the desk clerk and left the doctor's office.

The moral of the story: Worrying about a situation can only add more to the problem. It never solves the problem.

DOCTOR'S OFFICE

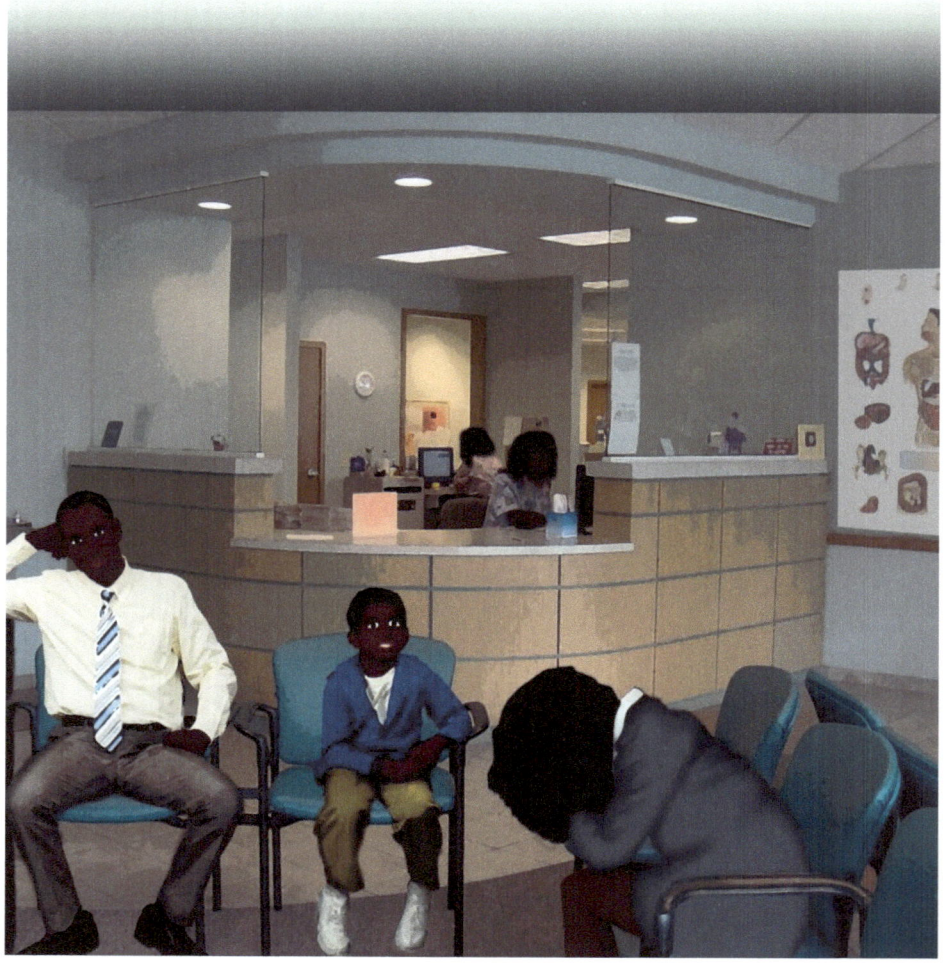

The Coincidence

It was the most puzzling day of his life. The awakening of dawn sprawled over the land, painting a screen on the trees. The few pin top stars blinked farewell to welcome a new day.

The promise of adventure awoke him. His eyes were wild, his mouth was half-open. In despair, Mr. Jackson gathered himself for a final heave and sat upright on his bed. He remained unclear as to what was the dream. Then he was alarmed as his cocks sounded their trumpets, and as they competed with the other villagers' cocks. The sounds of dogs, barking aggressively, and others with long, loud, wailing cries could be heard distinctly.

"Some relative or close friend must have been passed away." He got up laboriously. Then, he walked wistfully towards the doorway and closed the door gently behind him. The brilliant concert closed as millions of insects sounded off. The morning was a bit chilly and the sweet fragrance of wax apple blossoms pervaded the air. Mr. Jackson sauntered towards the Wax Apple plot. The redness of the wax apples, fresh with dew drops, met his droopy eyes.

Venturing a few yards farther, he caught sight of two unfamiliar persons. What business could these people have here? They both had briefcases.

"Hi," the medium, thick-set man greeted. "Nice place you have here," as he walked proudly with a half-smile to meet Mr. Jackson.

"Yes," Mr. Jackson replied.

Then he explained what the nature of their visit was. "We're planning to make this a paradise," explained the thick set man.

"What you mean by making this place a paradise?" asked Mr. Jackson.

"Well, sir........ What's the name?"

"Jackson."

"My colleague and I felt that it's an ideal place to construct a housing project and a food canning industry."

"I-I-I think the farm is acceptable as it is," Mr. Jackson responded.
"Wake up. It is time to stop being the sentimental type," the man retorted in an alarming voice.
Mr. Jackson sighed and looked at the vast area with distress. He walked a few frustrated steps through the carambola patch. As he plowed through the patch, the dry crisp leaves formed a carpet under his feet. Overhead, the hum of doves, hovering in the air, could be heard in steady swarms.

The land was bulldozed. Five hours later, the backhoe driver drilled the bucket into the soil, to a certain depth. He noticed the soil appeared strange. The colour of the soil was jet black and clammy.

"All my life I never, never saw the soil this colour." he said.

What could it be? The businessmen were looking at the plan and discussing it at the time. The bald-headed businessman, was trying to shield his head from the scorching sun. His eyes strayed. He then gathered all his vision into a concentrated spark. He could not believe his eyes. He drew it to the other man's attention.

Then the man said with a high-pitched voice, "It looks like we hit oil!"

The bald head man said, "Oil!" as if he never heard of oil before.

The thick-set man then sent out a radio call to report the oil discovery. An hour after, it was broadcast over the news media that oil was struck at "EVER GREENFARM."

That same day, Mr. Jackson bought a newspaper and he saw the headline: "EVER GREEN FARM STRUCK OIL!!!" On his way to the J and K Grocery parking lot, he saw a line that touched him. "J. Peterson claimed the land was owned by Francil and Shane Trod." Mr. Jackson was so upset, he raced to the farm. Meanwhile, the brothers were on the farm land looking on as the builders worked diligently.

"Look, you all get out of here!" Mr. Jackson demanded hastily as he panted.

"We have rights here," bellowed the brothers. "Furthermore, Mr. Franklyn Trod is our father," they said.

"What?" shouted Mr. Jackson.

"He is my father, too," replied Mr. Jackson.

Francil and Shane looked at each other in astonishment.

Eventually, Francil broke the silence and said, "Well! Well! It took this oil discovery for us to know that we are brothers!"

Then Mr. Jackson shook his head and said, "I wonder why dad never told me that I had brothers?"

Immediately, Shane blurted out "That is unusual, dad never seemed to be the secrecy type."

"Well, now you know," Francil said, as if he did not put anything past his father.

"I think we should all visit him now and confront him about this matter," Mr. Jackson said.

"It is too late, brother," Shane said.

"What you mean by that?" Mr. Jackson said in a puzzling way.

"I thought you knew," Francil stepped in and said.

"Dad passed away four days ago."

At once, Mr. Jackson's legs grew weak, and he started to weep uncontrollably.

It was as if he was short of breath now. His brothers held him and put him to sit on some dry leaves that formed a cushion under him.

A few minutes after, Mr. Jackson caught himself. He said in a low tone of voice, "It was not just the shock about my father's death, but it was the fact that we were not on good terms the last time we spoke. I cannot help but wonder if he forgave me and I did not get a chance to tell him how sorry I was about the situation."

Before any of the brothers could have responded, a car driver was driving a black car so fast that it left the air fogged with dust. As the driver approached them, the car screeched to a standstill. Then the driver shouted, "Mr. Jackson, I have a letter here for you!"

With stretched-out arms, Shane helped his brother up. Then Mr. Jackson quickened his pace towards the driver. For a moment, Mr. Jackson, said to himself, "I wonder who could be sending me a letter?"

As the driver stretched out his hand to give the letter Mr. Jackson saw that his father's name was on it and the letter, was posted a week before. Then the driver drove off. Instantly, Mr. Jackson ripped the envelope opened and he started to read.

Dear Son,

I hope that this letter meets you in good health. I just want you to know that I have forgiven you for what you did. I felt the urge for letting you know that I have forgiven you because I am dying from Cancer.

Love,

Dad

As Mr. Jackson finished reading the letter, he felt peace come over him and he was overwhelmed with joy that not even words could have expressed. Then he showed his brothers the letter as he hollered," Dad has forgiven me!"

As they caressed each other, they thanked God for bringing them together.

The moral of the story is: Secrets do come to light in due time.

Easy Come Easy Go

The wind-driven rain, had now slackened to a drizzle. Peter was feeling hungry, so he stopped and stepped inside a fast-food restaurant on the Bay Road. He sat down at a table and he took up the menu booklet and read it. He then ordered rice and mutton, along with a glass of lemonade.

As Peter glanced across the room, his eyes stumbled upon a long-time schoolmate. The name Reynold was formed, but not a sound came from his mouth. He swallowed hard and made a fresh start. Reynold's and his eyes met.

Reynold came over, folded his arms and stared directly at Peter. With a nervous movement, Reynold wiped his eyes with his coat sleeve. His mouth was still a little open.

Then Peter began crying. He made no attempt to stem the tears. They just ran down his face and he mopped them up with his handkerchief. Within a few seconds, Peter sprang from his seat and clung to Reynold like a magnet, as they laughed heartedly.

The waitress arrived with Peter's food. Peter and Reynold were seated and chatting away. Then the waitress told Peter that his bill was thirty-five dollars. Reynold continued speaking as though he did not hear the interruption.

"It is alright, Gwen, it is on me," Reynold said. "Boy, a yesterday self I asked Keith about you and he told me that he has not seen you for years now."

"Man, I spent fifteen years in prison, and I was released just two days ago." That very moment, Peter wanted to hold Reynold's attention, because the things he wanted to say that lay so heavily on his heart, needed Reynold's whole and undivided attention. "Prison was a nightmare. If you do not have the strength and courage, you cannot make it out of prison. You know, Rey, I always heard about prison, but now I had a firsthand experience for myself. What I supposed I wanted most, was to get a lot of money, which I did acquire. Then the thrill wore off; what's left? I also wanted to be famous, but not in the way it turned out, with my picture and name printed in the newspaper.

"PETER WIGLEY WAS FINED FOR POSSESSION OF HEROIN AND ALSO FOR TRAFFICKING IT".

Then I had more deals. Eventually, when I tried to come out of the deals, the police caught up with me again. Then I was sentenced to prison."

Reynold smiled inwardly. He felt Peter had learnt the hard way and now he was beginning to appreciate living one day at a time.

"And I am...." Reynold began to say, but Peter interrupted him.

"Enough about me. Tell me about you."

"Well, boy, I just opened this little restaurant here," Reynold said.

"So you working for somebody?" Peter asked.

"Boy, no. The restaurant is mine!"

By now, Peter had stopped eating, "Boy I happy for you," he said fighting down the irritation in his voice. "So these people helped set you up?" Peter asked Reynold, as his eyes searched his face. Peter knew vaguely that Reynold's family had money and that he was the only child.

"Yes, my family was very supportive of me," Reynold said.

"Boy, Rey, nice speaking to you," Peter said, rising suddenly. "I have to go, I have some business to take care of."

Reynold escorted Peter to the door and they bade each other farewell. Then Peter paused. He was moved by an impulse of tenderness. He glanced over his shoulder at Reynold, and he shambled away.

As Peter strolled down the street, "Boy no, the restaurant is mine," was all he could think about. He was rigid with pain. "Anyway, I am going to start over and become successful, too."

Gradually, as he vanished into the crowd of people strolling up the road, Peter said to himself, "What a mess I have made of my life. But hey, I know that I could prevent youths from walking the path I took in my early life. Perhaps, I can start by speaking to the youths in the schools."

The moral of the story: Be satisfied with what little you have until you get more.

The last Dollar

Thomas peered out the window into the night. Outside, the wind had built up to a dull growl.

Suddenly, his ears picked up a clattering noise. The noise seemed to reverberate in every part of his being. A picture of his mother in her coffin flashed across his mind, but he pushed it back into the subconscious, 'My mother is not going to die.' But the confidence he tried to put in his voice failed. His voice quaked a little. After a moment, Thomas managed to control the thought of losing his mother.

He sidled into his mother's bedroom. He stared at his mother for some moments before daring to open his mouth. His mother was unaware that she was being watched. She was lying on her box bed. Her frail hands were clasped. Her eyes were clamped shut. Her chapped lips were moving, but not a sound came from her mouth.

Not long after she, held her stomach and seemed to be short of breath. She looked so tired and helpless. He then advanced to her bed. Thomas framed words to utter and now as he opened his mouth to speak, his mother interrupted, "You look worried."

"Not really, mom," he answered as if he was not sure what he was saying.

Then she whispered, "I am going to tell you something I never told anyone. When I was young," she said as she rose, very shakily and feebly.

At that moment, the clattering sound began again as she held her stomach. Momentarily, he was stiffened with nerve. Then Thomas said, "Mom do you want me to get the doctor?"

"Son," then she paused. "I-I-I have the last twenty-five dollars. It is for you to help your four little sisters. Just bring mama a warm cup of bush tea," she said as she blinked away her tears.

Thomas quickened his pace towards the nearby drop-shed kitchen. Then he took out a small bundle of charcoals. He placed them in the car-rim coal pot and he wet a piece of cloth with kerosene oil. Then he struck the match. A puff of grey smoke climbed through the wooden window. Occasionally, when the wind direction shifted the smoke blew against him. As he fanned the fire with a piece of cardboard, he coughed, while his tiny eyes wept. Still he kept on fanning the fire like an automatic windmill. Yet there was no sign of the coal turning red.

Thomas flung on more kerosene oil on the charcoals. The kitchen was now pervaded with a white cloud of smoke. Again, he struck the match. A sound, 'poof' went off at once. The smoke turned into a blaze of fire with its tongue inches into the air. As Thomas fanned the blazing fire with all his might a whooshing sound erupted. Eventually, the fire began to spark like fireworks. Then the coals turned from black to red. Thomas was now at ease a little. He then placed the teapot on the fire, with a cup of water. In no time, the water was hot enough to draw the basil bush.

As Thomas poured the tea in a cup he said, "I better quicken my pace. My mother must be waiting on me."

Thomas thrust his way into the room. He said, "Mom I brought your tea, just the way you like it." Thomas did not hear his mother answer. He called again, but this time with pain in his voice. "Mom, I brought your tea." Still no answer. Thomas froze in his tracks.

Within a few moments, Thomas felt his mother forehead. Her forehead felt as if she was in a furnace. Thomas wet a piece of cloth and placed it on his mother's forehead. She was now rambling in her talk Thomas was frightened more than ever now.

Suddenly, his mother opened her eyes. Then she grumbled, "Who are you?" Thomas' mind was distant now. "My own mother does not recognize me." He started to think what would happen to him and his four sisters. Then he stared at his mother and said, "I am only eleven, how am I going to look after my sisters?"

Thomas hit the floor with depression. He thought while overwhelmed by frustration, "My mother seemed not to be any better. I have done all I could possibly do." He felt helpless. Then Thomas said, "Well I am going to get the doctor for mom. I am going to take twenty-four dollars from the twenty-five dollars."

Thomas then started preparing the house for the doctor's visit. He had a basin with water, soap and a clean towel laid out for the doctor.

The slanting beam of light was now appearing in his mother's room. After he finished organizing the room, Thomas pelted down the road. He was down the last stretch off the dry dusty road towards the doctor's house.

Within twenty-five minutes, Thomas knocked on the door.

He was a stocky loud- voiced doctor. Thomas heard the loud voice saying, "I am coming. Who is at the door?"

Thomas answered, "Thomas!"

"Okay sonny boy I am on my way." As Dr. Caines opened the door, he said, "Sonny boy, good morning. How may I help?"

Thomas tried to stem the tears before he swallowed hard and said, "My mother is terribly sick. I want you to come to the house and examine her, please."

"Okay, sonny, boy try and take it easy, I will be over shortly."

Just as Thomas nearly reached home, Dr. Caines followed behind with lightning speed. Thomas was astonished and delighted when he noticed the doctor reached very quickly to his home. Thomas beckoned Dr. Caines to come inside. Then he escorted him to his mother's bedroom. All the girls were around her now.

Then Dr. Caines sat on the wooden chair next to the bed. "How are you, Ms. Jackson?" The doctor asked inquisitively.

Ms. Jackson grumbled, "For days I just kept on coughing terribly."

Then the doctor examined Ms. Jackson as he scratched nervously at his fluffy white beard. He paused then said, "You have bronchitis, Ms. Jackson."

Before Ms. Jackson could respond, Jamie, Ms. Jackson's last daughter interrupted, "Dr. Caines, what is bronchitis?"

"That is a very good question, little girl," the doctor responded. "Mommy just has an infection in the tubes that go to her lungs. I will just write a paper for her to get some Antibiotics. Mommy will be alright in no time."

Then her mother gestured yes, nodding her head up and down.

Dr. Caines wrote the prescription, while pressing on his knees. Then he said, "Thomas, you could get the medication for sixty-five dollars at Valu Pharmacy," as he extended his hands to give Thomas the prescription.

"I will go, doctor," Thomas said at once, relieved that Dr. Caines said nothing about his mother going to the hospital. Then Thomas paid the doctor's fee of twenty-four dollars.

"Ms. Jackson you really have a great little fellow."

"Yes, he is a great little fellow."

Thomas just smiled and pelted out the door to get the medicine

Suddenly, Dr. Caines suggested, "Thomas we can walk down the road together?"

While Thomas was waiting, out of the blue, he said, "Lord I have the last dollar to buy my mother's medication. How in the world I am going to look after my mother and sisters. Lord, please help."

Within a few seconds, Dr. Caines came down the steps to meet Thomas. As they walked briskly down the road, Dr. Caines said, "You know, son, I can tell you really love your mother. You really the man of the house."

Gradually, the doctor reached his hairy hands in his jean trousers pocket. Then he said, "You might need an extra dollar to help your mother get back on her feet. So take this sixty dollars."

Instantly, Thomas eyes lit up. He never saw so much money in a large amount. Thomas' mouth opened. His throat was clamped. Then he stared at Dr. Caines delightfully. "Thank you Dr. Caines," Thomas repeated over a period of time.

"You are welcome, son," Dr. Caines said as he shook Thomas' hand firmly.

They were now approaching the junction in the road.

As they reached the junction in the road, they bade each other farewell and departed into different directions.

Thomas was a few blocks away from the towering building. The pharmacy was at the bottom floor.

Thomas had to enter a little hallway with benches running horizontally along the side. At the extreme end, there was a window like the one in a railway ticket office. Thomas knocked at the window. A lanky, bearded-looking man opened the window. Without waiting for Thomas to complete what he was saying, the man grabbed the prescription from Thomas. Then he slammed the shutter down without a word. Thomas waited for almost fifteen minutes, and still there was no sight of the man. Then Thomas said, "Maybe they ran out of the medication my mother wanted." He waited another fifteen minutes, but still no sign of the man. Thomas took three frustrated steps backward. Then he shifted his weight from one foot to the other. Just as Thomas was about to knock again, the man opened the squeaky shutter.

Then he said, "Little boy, you just got the last of the medication."

Thomas sighed with relief. Then he said, "Thank you," with a broad grin across his face. Within a split of a second, Thomas dashed out the pharmacy.

When Thomas got back into the house, he shouted, "Mom I got the medication! Mom I got the medication!" Thomas greeted his mother with a warm smile.

She smiled back. Ms. Jackson did not have much schooling.

Thomas read what was written on the medication: "Take two tablets every eight hours until finished." He gave his mother two tablets," Then he told her, "Mom, every eight hours take two tablets," as he illustrated with two of his fingers, "until the medication is finished."

With a big smile on his face, Thomas said, "Mom you do not have to worry about how we are going to get food to eat."

His mother looked startled.

Thomas paused for a moment, then he said, "Mom, this morning when Dr. Caines told me to wait, he gave me sixty dollars."

Then his mother said, "God answers prayers."

Then Thomas echoed what his mother said, "God answers prayers."

His mother hugged him tightly. Then she said, "God bless you, son," as she ran her long slender fingers through his soft, jet black, curly hair.

Within a matter of days, Ms. Jackson was back on her feet. Everything practically went back to normal. After all, God does answer prayers.

The moral of the story is: God has a way of providing our needs by using others as his vessels.

The Bullies

I tried to explain, but they just would not listen to me. I was called a 'waste; I kept silent, striving to offer no excuse to worsen the situation.

Suddenly, Ricaldo burst into the classroom. Then Reo said, "Ricaldo, wait a minute, let me take care of this 'waste'."

"So 'waste', you think you will ever turn out to be somebody?" Reo asked in a slow, sadistic voice.

"I do not know," I grumbled, my head turned away from him.

"If I was a waste, I would hate myself," Reo whispered.

I kept my mouth shut. I was furious.

"But I am not surprised, 'waste' does not mind being 'waste'." he said sarcastically and laughed.

I ignored him. Ricaldo was staring at me closely, and then I saw them exchange glances.

Ricaldo soon edged over where I was seating and he blocked my view. He folded his arms and stared at me solemnly. I glanced from one to the other, sensing trouble. I knew that there was no way out. I was now fenced in. My lungs were aching. I kept seeing a picture of them beating me.

Suddenly, Ricaldo grabbed me by the collar, with his right hand, ramming my head against the classroom wall. I wanted to pray but, I could not think straight. "Oh, you think that you are going to get away this time," he bellowed.

My legs shook violently. Perspiration streamed down my face.

"Reo told me that you were the one who told Mr. Hull that I punctured his car wheels," Ricaldo snapped.

I stared at Ricaldo, his face was like metal. I opened my mouth to speak, to assure him that I was innocent, but my throat was clamped. I moved my lips; there was no sound.

He raised his left hand. Ricaldo had a knife. He waved it in front of my face. My heart lurched sickeningly.

Everything and everybody I had ever known flashed through my mind instantly. I did not want to die. I began shaking. Then Ricaldo shouted, "Stop shaking, you stingy waste!" But I only shook for the better.

"Now waste, I will let you go, but if you ever tell anyone, I will get even with you. Now get out of here!" He did not have to repeat himself. I dashed out the room.

On my way down the hall, I saw Mr. Jones, the Deputy Principal. I wanted to report the incident to Mr. Jones, but the thought of what Ricaldo and Reo would do to me stopped me, So I just said, "Hello," and went my way.

While the bullying was going on, Theo was in the next room videotaping the incident. Theo stood in the room until he heard no sound coming from the room. Then he picked his way gingerly to the doorway to make sure that the way was clear. He tiptoed out in the hallway and he glanced in many directions to make sure no one saw him leaving the room. Theo was sure now that no one saw him, so he strolled down the hallway as if nothing just happened.

Suddenly, fear engulfed him. Then he said to himself, "I want to report this incident, but I am afraid of those bullies because they are twice my size," Theo swallowed hard and then he said, as if he just got a bright idea, "If I do not report this incident, I am just as bad as the bullies."

As Theo turned the corner towards the Principal's office, he saw the Deputy Principal talking with a teacher. Theo froze in his tracks a few steps away from them. Mr. Jones realized Theo's presence. Then he said to the teacher that they would talk some more later. Mr. Jones knew that Theo was the type of person who was very quiet and most of the time when he had something to say he would be very timid, so he wanted to make it easier on him.

"Theo, boy, how are you today?"

"Instead of answering the question Theo stammered and said, "Mr._ Mr._Mr._ Jones."

"What is it son?" Mr. Jones asked in a concerned way.

"I_ I_ I have a video to show you," he said as he stretched out his small hands to give it to the Deputy Principal.

As Mr. Jones looked at the video, a shock wave hit him. He was now raging inside, but he tried not to show it to the little boy.

Then, in a low tone of voice, the Deputy Principal said, "Thanks, son," as he gave Theo a tap on his back. Within a second, they departed from each other.

All the way the Deputy was going, he said to himself, "Bullying will not be tolerated in this school, I will give the harshest penalty to this problem."

On second thought, the Deputy Principal said, "I better go home and sleep on this matter and deal with it the next day."

The next day, the Deputy Principal sent and called the bullies in the office.

He told the boys in a stern voice, "Take a seat." Then the Deputy Principal started replaying the video.

At once, the boys looked at each other astonished. The Deputy Principal halted the video.

The room was silent now. Then Mr. Jones cleared his throat and said, "Anyone of you has anything to say?"

The boys just watched the Deputy Principal for a little while and they pulled down their heads and said, "No, sir."

"Well, I spoke to your parents a while ago, as well as whatsApped the video to them, and they all agreed to give both of you the severest punishment. Both of your parents have decided that none of you will be going to Disney World for the summer vacation. Instead, you all will do charity work, such as being assigned to the hospital to look after the elderly patients."

Out of the blue, Ricaldo burst out, "My mommy and daddy cannot do that!"

Then Reo joined in and said, "Uncle Neil will never do something like that."

The Principal interrupted and said, "Boys I have not completed what I wanted to say. Also, both of you will attend summer camps to teach the children that bullying can have a negative impact on children, as well as sharing with them the great price you all had to pay for bullying a student in your school."

Then the principal added, "That is all I have to say, and I hope that you all will learn from this lesson."

Within a few seconds, the room went silent again. Then the Principal broke the silence and said, "You all may go now."

The boys stood up. They took a few frustrated steps as they made their way out of the principal's office.

The moral of the story is: Help others to excel in life rather than try to destroy them.

The Shortcut Home

The day was overcast and cold. It felt like it was going to rain.

Sophie, Carelle and Teshelle were coming from modelling class. Suddenly, Sophie blurted out, "Girls, suppose we cut through the Independence Square instead of walking all the way around to our houses?"

"Come on," Carelle said to Teshelle, who was a little hesitant.

Eventually Teshelle said, "Alright, let us go."

As they strolled into the Independence Square, Sophie had a feeling that someone was walking behind them. As she glanced over her shoulder, she did not see anyone.

The person had dodged behind a tree to conceal himself.

Then she said to herself, "Girl keep your over active imagination under control; your friends will think you are hallucinating."

They were four yards from Carelle's house now. Sophie kept on looking back. This time she, saw the stocky man with dark shades on his face. She pondered for a moment, and then she said, "Carelle and Teshelle, I think someone is following us."

At once Carelle said, "Sophie, that is nonsense," as she stole a glance backward.

Then Teshelle said, "You do not have to talk to her like that; maybe what she is saying is right."

"Listen, Teshelle," Carelle said, "you do not have to agree with me."

The man was a few steps behind them now. Carelle could actually hear his footsteps.

He walked briskly behind them and said, "All of you continue walking as if nothing strange is happening."

As Teshelle looked back, she recognized the dark shades, khaki jacket and the black boots with metal reinforced tips. It was the same man Sophie saw earlier. He had something in his hand that looked like a gun.

Then he said, "Continue walking until I say stop."

Suddenly, Sophie's feet buckled under her.

The man muttered, "Just keep moving."

They were now in an area where there was dense bush. The man then said, "Stop!"

All of the girls stopped, except Carelle.

"Girl you hear me!" the man barked. Carelle still continued, dragging her feet.

The man called out to her again. His voice now took on the bluntness of finality. "Girl, I have a gun; It has live bullets in it. I can shoot you." Carelle halted in her tracks.

"Now we talking business. And from now on, everyone do as I say, or else," he said as he waved the gun in front of them. The man looked at Carelle and said, "Take off your leather jackets and your diamond earrings."

Without hesitating, Carelle took out the earrings and took off the jacket.

Then he said, "Put the earrings in the jacket pocket and toss it to me."

That she did.

"You with the fancy-coloured finger nails, take off that gold chain," he said to Janelle. He walked around her. Then he asked, "What else you have to give?"

"Nothing, sir," Janelle said in a frightened manner.

"You with the fancy hairdo, give me your leather bag."

Teshelle's lungs were aching. She kept seeing a picture of her family. She was shaking violently. She wanted to pray, but she could not think straight.

"You cannot talk? Are you a mute?" he said to Teshelle.

Teshelle's bubbling eyes were stuck on the gun. She tried to open her mouth, but her throat was gripped tightly.

The man was getting impatient and said to her, "What happened, cat got your tongue? I said all you have to do is do as I say."

Her heart lurched sickeningly. It hurt, and she wanted to scream.

He raised the gun and said, "Okay, you do not want to give me the bag, I will take it myself, then."

At that point, Carelle and Sophie begged, "Teshelle, do as the man say!"

Then the man said, "Girls, move back three steps from that girl."

Carelle and Sophie took the three steps back.

"Stay right there," the man said abruptly. He now turned his attention back to Teshelle. As he advanced towards her, Teshelle shook violently. He attempted to grab her bag, but Teshelle clutched her bag. Within a blink of an eye, he gave her a back hand slap. He pushed her slightly, then he said, "I am not afraid to shoot you!"

Immediately, Teshelle loosened her grip on the bag. Shortly after that Teshelle's life began to flash in front of her. In that instant, she knew that she had so much to live for. She did not want to die.

He opened the bag. He took out a brush, some makeup and a comb which he tossed into the air. Her purse, he opened .There was five hundred dollars in cash, which she had to pay down for her laptop computer. "Look what my girl has here! Five hundred dollars in cash," he said smiling.

He said, "I am going to let you all go, but if you all were to ever report this incident to the police or anyone, all of your families will go six feet." Within seconds, he vanished from the scene.

Teshelle moved to get out of there yet she felt as if she was still standing and peering into the man's face. Then she sobbed hysterically. Her friends tried to comfort her. She cried, "Leave me alone, for next time. I mean there will not be a next time.

"So you're blaming us now?" Carelle questioned.

"Nobody is blaming anybody. Carelle suggested the shortcut back home and all of us agreed. All of us wanted to take the shortcut through the Independence Square," Sophie said.

"Yes, but when I said I saw a man following us, Carelle said it was nonsense," Teshelle quickly followed up in response to Sophie

Carelle jumped into the conversation and said, "Teshelle, if you just had done what the man asked you to do, then you would not have been hurt."

"Let us stop arguing. The important thing is we are alive," Sophie insisted.

They were approaching Narelle's house now. Suddenly, Sophie asked, "Teshelle are you going to tell your parents?

"Yes," Teshelle said bluntly. "I will walk the remaining block back home, alone."

One of her friends said, "Okay, suit yourself."

As Teshelle opened the gate her father was on the veranda in the rocking chair. Her father saw the bruise.

"Darling what happened to your cheek?" he asked as he peered into his daughter's face.

Teshelle remembered what the man said, if she was to tell the police or anyone, then her entire family will go six feet. "I...I....I was not watching where I was going. I butt into a metal sign post."

Her dad hugged her and carried her inside. He put cubes of ice in a piece of white cloth and held it to her left cheek. Then he kissed her on the forehead. Eventually he said, "Darling next time try and be more careful. Thank God your bruise is not that bad."

From that day, Teshelle never took another short cut home.

The moral of the story: Shortcut can lead to long-term problems, and it may be difficult to solve them.

Gone So Long

The fair day had flown by, and a dull cover of clouds had blown up from the west. Rachel was waiting in the J&K restaurant to meet her two brothers and two sisters who lived in England.

She was waiting for well over a half hour now. Rachel was tired of sitting and waiting. She got up laboriously, went outside and ended up wandering around the perimeter of the restaurant. It began to drizzle again, driving her at last back in the restaurant. She took refuge in the ladies room and renewed her make-up.

Within a half of an hour, Rachel presented herself at the dining terrace. The slim, well-dressed waitress escorted her to a discrete corner table. It was one away from a set for eight with a reservation slip sticking out of a glass. By now the rest of the room was full. Still she could not see her brothers and sisters anywhere. Rachel could not remember whether she decided it would be better to enter and surprise them. Perhaps it would be better to be there when they come in and give them a smile. Rachel was so confused. She gulped down a drink.

As she scanned the room, she watched a lady say something to her lady-friend, something obviously flattering. Then a little wave of recognition came from the lady. It made Rachel feel good, even though she was acutely unaware of the appraising and evaluating going on behind those cheerful, welcoming expressions.

The lady who laid eyes on Rachel first, got up and came toward her. The lady leaned down and kissed Rachel and whispered, "Pleased to meet you." Then she straightened up and in a more formal way she asked Rachel if she would like to join them.

Just as Rachel stood up, she saw her brothers and sisters facing her. All of them were heading towards the same table. There was a brief shuffle while a tenth place was set, and the lady's friend shifted. Then a chair was brought.

Lisa, Rachel's last sister said, "Rachel the lady who brought you over is a friend of ours, Ms. Gardener, and the other lady is Ms. Lake."

Then Rachel said, "It is a pleasure meeting you, Ms. Lake."

"Likewise," Ms. Lake answered.

Rachel had a lengthy conversation with her sisters and brothers, along with their friends. While T'rone Rachel's first brother was telling them what happened to him on the way to the restaurant, Rachel stole a glance at Ms. Gardener. Ms. Gardener, looked the way Rachel hoped to look when she got to fifty or sixty years old. Ms. Gardener's face was still gleaming with youth.

Gradually, Rachel's thought shifted. Then she said to herself, "No one mentioned anything about mother, so I am not going to ask. Maybe she does not even think about me."

Suddenly, another lady was heading in their direction. The lady resembled Rachel in many ways, with long black hair, almond slittered eyes, small nose and lips painted with rosy lipstick, and dangling earring suiting her oval smooth dark face. They were staring at each other as if they wanted to dive into each other.

Immediately, everyone at the table started laughing as if they were tickled by someone. Rachel laughed a little, too, though she did not get the joke. As the lady reached to them, she took the seat opposite Rachel. Rachel was still staring at the lady. Everyone at the table started laughing again.

Then Hahanna, Rachel's second sister asked half smiling, "Rachel, who does the lady look like?"

"Me," Rachel answered abruptly.

"So do you know who the person is?" Lisa asked.

"No," Rachel answered abruptly again.

Everyone started laughing again. There was only the resemblance Rachel seemed to recognize. She drummed her fingers irritably on the table. She felt as if a screen had been interposed between herself and the exact memory she was searching for. Then she pressed her eyes shut, wanting to squeeze forth the specific recollection like water from a sponge. Nothing came. Rachel finished her other drink. It happened very rarely, to be sure, but this was not the first time her powers of recollection had come up dry.

Suddenly, Jason her younger, brother blurred out. "She is your mother!"

Rachel was startled. Eventually, when Rachel's brother's words got through the doubt that fogged her mind, she plunged into her mother's arms. She sobbed happily. In between her tears, she said, "Mom, I used to say that when I get to see you, I will never talk to you. You turned off left me a baby with my grandmother and never looked back."

Then her mother, Gwendolyn, said, "I had my reason for leaving you with your grandmother."

"Back then, I thought it was the best I could have done. I wished I could take it all back, but I cannot." She paused for a brief moment. Then she smiled in a way that made Rachel feel she was in pain. "I was young and thought I could have taken on the world. I was very much in love with your father. He was ten years older than I was. By the time I was fourteen, I got pregnant with you. He asked me if I was sure that you were his. I said yes. But he could not accept it. Then he stopped seeing me and he ran off, and left me for another woman. I was depressed. My mother then told me that I got myself pregnant and I will have to look after my child myself. I was all alone and scared. At first I thought about having an abortion. But for some reason I did not have the guts to abort you.

However, I carried you for the nine months. I remembered the day you were born. It was like yesterday."

Rachel looked at her mother. Her eyes were gray, she thought. Storm gray: the sky before thunder. Rachel looked into her mother's eyes. She wanted to drown in them.

"At first I thought I could manage you," her mother continued, as if she had a load pressing down on her stomach and she wanted to get the weight of her stomach. "But most of the time you kept on crying and crying for hours. After a while, it was like you were driving me crazy. I did not know how to comfort you. Then one day I told my mother that I am going to town to get something for you. I left you with my mother. I never returned. Instead, I bought a ticket and left for England."

Then Gwendolyn said, "Enough about me, tell me about you."

"Well," Rachel said before adding, "There is nothing much to say. I am a mother now at sixteen," Rachel said as she bowed her head.

Within a few minutes, Lisa interrupted and said, "Let us look at the menu now and order something to drink and eat."

All of them then ordered what they wanted and they had a jolly good time.

A few days later, Gwendolyn organized a trip for Rachel to go to England.

Rachel had one of the greatest moments of her life. She was able to see what outside of St. Kitts looked like for the first time.

The moral of story: Sometimes people have to walk out of someone's life to give the person a better chance in life.

Gone But Not Forgotten

As Kelvin lay on the couch, he opened and read his mail. The bank statement showed that he was in the red. He was furious. He sprang to his feet. As he made an effort to control his agitation, he saw the postcards on the line. When he stared at them, he was filled with thoughts. Although there was no one displayed on the postcards, it was as if there was someone looking right back at him.

Suddenly, his mind flashed to the time when he opened the envelope and skimmed through his wife's medical report. Kelvin spotted the word "Cancer". For a second, he did not believe what he saw. On a second attempt, he read the report, word for word, but the word 'cancer' was still there. Tears began to leak down his cheeks. Kelvin was speechless.

When Kelvin used to visit Clara's bedside in the hospital, she had a calm confidence about the future and very deep faith in God. Sometimes, Kelvin used to cry and say, "Clara you have to fight, for our sake."

Despite the terrible tragedy she was facing, she dried his tears with her hands. She paused for a second. Then she told him, "Kelvin, weep no more. We will see each other again"

For a second, he dismissed what Clara said as delusional, but at the same time he did not want to believe what he was thinking either.

Then she stared at him inquisitively, before she uttered a word. "I know you do not believe in the Bible, so you might not understand right away, where I am coming from. I pray that one day you will consider knowing God."

Kelvin sighed. Then he said, "You know, darling, sometimes faith just withers away."

"Explain what you mean to me, honey?"

"Clara, there is something I never told you."

"Honey, you know you can talk to me."

"Yes, darling, but I do not want to burden you now."

But she insisted because she wanted to know what was on her husband's mind.

At first he hesitated, and then he let it out. "Since I was a child, my doubts and uncertainties about God fluctuated, and my disbelief grew. As weak as my faith was, my father's death was a severe blow to my faith. Despite the fact that I prayed and prayed to God to let him survive, he still died."

Clara listened keenly as she digested what her husband was saying. Tears began to sting his eye lids. She then said, "Honey your experience is not unusual. No matter what happened in life, there comes a time when you have to lay down your burdens and praise the Lord."

"Yes darling, but I blamed myself up to this very day. If I did not forget my asthmatic pump, my father would not have had to turn back home to get it. We would not have been in the wrong place at the right time. That car should not have hit us head on," Kelvin said in between his sobbing. "My father was not supposed to get that blow to his head." He calmed down a bit.

"Honey, unfortunately, we may feel guilty at times without really being guilty. What happened to you because you had forgotten your asthmatic pump, you allowed legitimate remorse to come over your mistake. Then you started to feel ashamed and ended up punishing yourself unnecessarily."

"For years I kept silent. It was like my bones wore out through my groaning. Now letting it out eased my emotional pain. I am at peace with myself."

"Honey, I am glad that I was of some help to you," she said. Then they clung to each other.

"Good bye, honey." he said.

"Good bye, darling,"

On his way out, she called him back and told him, "Do not forget to trust and believe in the Lord. He will see you through good times and bad times."

For a moment, it was as if Kelvin was in a different world, and now he had come back to himself. Then he said, "Clara I am going to do just as you told me, to trust and believe in the Lord, and he will see me through good times, and bad times."

Suddenly, he flung himself to the floor, and as he knelt with tears in his eyes, he looked up in the high roof ceiling and prayed, "Lord I surrender myself to you, forgive me for my trespasses."

Then he held his wife's had with a firm grip and said, "Darling, thank you for helping me to finally surrender my life to Jesus."

The moral of the story: The memories of someone can still have an impact on someone else, although he or she passes away.

The Trainee Pilot

The sun shone brightly, while white pillowy clouds raced across the steel-blue sky. Benneth and his other air force colleagues were to make a mock attack on their own airfield.

Nearly an hour before Benneth's training, he was at the air force base. He was using the remaining time to review the instructions for his pilot test. Suddenly, a deafening roar and a downdraft was heard. It was an aircraft out of the west. The pilot settled it on the helipad. The blades ceased to chop the air. Then there was complete silence.

Benneth peeped out the window. It was a gigantic helicopter. He was startled. It was much bigger than those Benneth was accustomed to. They had been delayed for well over twenty-five minutes now.

From the door of the air force division, their squadron leader, Victor, had been keeping track of the incoming aircraft. As the engine noise died away, Victor breathed a sigh of relief. He hustled back into the airy room where the trainees were. Victor clapped his hands and said, "Show time, boys."

They briskly walked outside to the planes. "All yours, boys," Victor said, saluting the trainees.

Then a lanky flight sergeant handed over life vests and helmets to them. Benneth looked at his watch. It was 11:45 a.m.

Victor helped the trainees buckle up and plugged in.

Benneth began to work the knobs, gauges and levers. The blades started to turn in swooping, awkward slices.

For twenty minutes, the trainees from the Indian Air force had flown west at a height of eight thousand (8000) feet. The trainees were flying on their squadron leader's left. They were waiting patiently for the command to turn to starboard.

Suddenly, the order came. As Benneth moved his controls, one of his comrades gave a violent shudder. Benneth was experiencing trouble. He was turned nose down and began a bullet-like dive for the forest below. Benneth throttled back. Earlier, in photographic details, the forest had looked like a soft green velvet carpet. Now it had a menacing appearance. Benneth was numb with horror. His eyes turned a little when he saw a thin silver ribbon. It was a river.

With force, he struggled with the controls. They felt like they were bolted in position. From thirty-four thousand feet, he had already fallen to half that height. All he could have thought of was, "I am going to crash! I am going to crash! Nothing could save me. Nothing could save me!"

Suddenly, he roused from his paralysing thoughts. A voice in his earphones gripped him. It was his squadron leader calling. "Benneth, fire your ejector. Benneth, fire your ejector! At once....over, do you hear me?"

Benneth was so shaken up, he was confused now. He could not remember which lever to push. Then in a panicky voice he said, "Victor, which lever!"

"Push down the red lever," Victor said.

At once Benneth pushed down the ejector lever. Instantly, he was ejected from the cockpit. Within seconds, his parachute opened. At this point, time changed for Benneth. Not in slow motion, but as if each second, each fragment of time was a separate slide.

Within minutes the crashing plane came down with lighting speed. Almost at once, dark billowing, thrusting smoke painted the air. Seconds later, the plane was engulfed in a blazing, fierce fire. It swallowed up everything in its path.

Suddenly, Benneth realized his oxygen was going low. He was now trying more than ever to land in a clearing. Eventually, he landed in a nearby cornfield that formed a cushion under him. He was lucky, because a few yards ahead there were high tension electricity lines.

As he crashed into the cornfield, the birds in the nearby trees flew in different directions, screaming and squawking in fear. Benneth began to pray on his knees. "Lord, I am angry that I failed my test. But I am thankful, beyond the shadow of doubt that you brought me through this horrific ordeal."

The moral of the story: Never lose hope. No matter the situation, you may just inspire an entire generation.

Visit **www.empressstanley.com**
For more information

www.globalcomputerfranchise.com

Affiliated with:

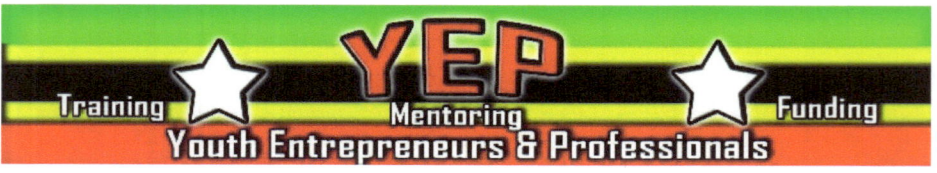

Y.E.P is an organization that helps entrepreneurs to publish their passions, proficiencies and products. Your support will help others!

1-305-381-1040 U.S.A/International
Nevis Street, Basseterre
St. Kitts

Acknowledgements

The publication of this collection of short stories entitled; **"An Insight into Life"** is a dream come through. My deepest gratitude is first and foremost to the almighty God. Without Him, this book would not have materialized.

Many thanks to my manager and close friend, Mr. Sanjay Caires, for his support.

My father and mother, Mr. Dodridge Huggins, Ms. Cassilda Stanley and my siblings for their support.

Mr. Leroy Pemberton for editing this work. He has also been a source of inspiration during the time that he taught me English.

Mrs. Angela Woodley has made suggestions to enhance the book.

Mr. Michael Blake for providing editorial support.

Willett's Photo Studio for designing the book cover.

Mr. Eustace Martin was very supportive in typing the manuscript.

Ms. Vernalderine Francis has been helpful in collaborating with me to create unique graphic pictures to capture specific moments in the stories.

Last but not least, thanks to my relatives, teachers, friends, students and well-wishers for their encouragement.

About the author

Empress Stanley is an ambitious, primary school teacher with eight (8) years experience. Also, she is an entrepreneur, vice president of Youth Entrepreneurs and Professionals (Y.E.P) and the Manager of Global Computer Franchise. She was born in St. Kitts and raised in the parish of St. Peter's, in an area called Fountain.

At a very early age, she had a passion for learning. Her early education started at the St.Peter's Primary School, now renamed Dean Glasford Primary School. She started her secondary education at the Basseterre Junior High School, now renamed Washington Archibald High School, and her secondary education ended at the Basseterre Senior High School.

Later, Ms. Stanley went on to the Clarence Fitzroy Bryant College where she acquired her early tertiary education.

After graduating from college, she had a deeper desire to assist young people, so she started writing short stories that focused mostly on issues young people encounter in life.

Also, she taught voluntarily at the Basseterre High School to help the first formers in the lower grades.

Shortly after that, Ms. Stanley was employed by the Epworth Maurice Hillier Memorial Junior School Board as a teacher. Within a few months of her employment at the school, Ms. Stanley enrolled at the University of the West Indies open Campus, in St. Kitts, to pursue a Bsc. in Management Studies. Upon completion of her studies, she obtained a Bsc. in Management Studies with Honours.

Currently, she is pursuing an MBA in Law at Anglia Ruskin University in England. Afterwards, she intends to pursue studies to bring her closer to her career goal of becoming a corporate lawyer.